Introducing Bookbinding

Introducing Bookbinding

Ivor Robinson

Oxford Polytechnic Press 1984

Editors: Claire Brown, Anne Fairclough,
Sarah Goodwin, Matthew Graham

Design and Production: Mary Hoare, Peter Jones,
Toni Langford, Nicky Postuma, Steven Siddle

Publicity and Sales: Rosemary Allen, Susan Day,
Anne Fairclough, Diana Holmes

First published by B. T. Batsford Ltd, London
in conjunction with Watson-Guptill Publications,
New York 1968.
This revised edition first published by
Oxford Polytechnic Press 1984.
Photographs by Ian Ross.
© Ivor Robinson 1968, 1984
ISBN 0 902692 25 9

British Library Cataloguing in Publication Data
Robinson, Ivor
    Introducing Bookbinding.—2nd ed.
    1. Bookbinding-Handbooks, manuals, etc.
    I. Title
6. 86.3   Z266

Text set in 14 on 15pt CRTronic Garamond at Oxford
Polytechnic Press, Headington, Oxford OX3 0BP.
Printed by Cotswold Press Ltd, Stanton Harcourt Road,
Eynsham, Oxford OX8 1JB on Huntsman Super White
Cartridge 115 gsm.
Bound at Paperback Binders of Abingdon, Oxon.

DEDICATION

For Hilary and Martin

And in memory of Eric Burdett, teacher of bookbinding at Bournemouth College of Art and Southampton College of Art between the years 1936 and 1968; and of John Richardson, teacher of bookbinding at London College of Printing and at the Northwestern Polytechnic between the years 1949 and 1979

ACKNOWLEDGEMENTS

6

To the First Edition

The author wishes to thank the Principal of the Oxford College of Technology and the Head of its School of Design, for permission to photograph equipment within the bookbinding department of the college and to show examples of the work of its students.
Oxford 1968

To the Second Edition

Since the first edition of *Introducing Bookbinding* was published the Oxford College of Technology has become the Oxford Polytechnic. The author is greatly indebted to the Publisher of the Oxford Polytechnic Press, and to those staff and students of Publishing whose interest and enthusiasm have resulted in this second edition. The work of some of the students directly concerned with the production is shown in those illustrations additional to the first edition and included on pages 58 to 62.
Oxford 1984

CONTENTS

INTRODUCTION

Bookbinding is an artistic craft of great antiquity, and at the same time a highly mechanised modern industry. The division between craft and industry is not so wide, however, as might at first be imagined. Indeed, it is interesting to observe that the three main problems presented to the mass-production bookbinder of today, with his automated lines of machinery, are those that confronted the medieval craftsman. The first problem is still how to hold together the leaves of a book; the second, how to protect those leaves once they are held together; and the third, how to identify and/or decorate the protective cover. These three problems are as fundamental now as they were during the early centuries of the craft. They are normally solved by a careful analysis of all the variables: these include consideration of the size of book, thickness of the book, type of paper or other text material and its make-up, value of the text, particular requirements related to style and use, the expected life span of the book, the number of books to be bound and factors concerned with the economics of the total binding task.

The purpose of this present work is to offer an introduction to tools, equipment and materials of the craft together with sequential demonstration of basic bookbinding skills likely to be within the scope of an average school, college or similar miscellaneous hand bindery.

I.R.

GLOSSARY

Forwarding the binding of a book up to the stage of lettering or the visual treatment of its cover.

Finishing the lettering or other visual treatment of the book cover.

Section the basic component of the body of a book, formed by folding a sheet of plain or printed paper into its subdivisions.

Leaf a single piece of paper hinged at the binding edge, usually formed when the book edges are cut and the section folds or bolts are removed.

Page one side of a leaf, either recto or verso.

Back the binding edge of a book.

Back-edge those parts of section, leaves and boards presented to the binding edge.

Foredge (fore-edge) the edge of leaves and boards opposite to the back-edge.

Head the top edge of leaves and boards.

Tail the bottom edge of leaves and boards.

Endpaper leaves variously formed and constructed which protect the first and last sections and provide an inner link between the body of a book and its boards.

Front board the board which protects the beginning of a book.

Off board the board which protects the end of a book.

Square the part of a board which extends beyond and protects the edges of the leaves.

Spine that part of the cover of a book which protects the back.

Joint the point of hinge between the body of a book, its boards, and its spine.

Case the cover of a book made separately from its body and joined to the latter as a final operation, as opposed to traditional binding structures in which the boards are attached to the body before the covering material is applied.

THE BINDERY

Bookbinding can best be carried out in a room with good even light and a water source, sink and washing facilities in the room or nearby.

A bench of about 72 x 30 inches (180 x 75cm) provides minimum working area for one person. The bench height should be approximately 36 inches (90cm), thus allowing certain operations to be performed standing. A stool is required for operations carried out at the bench in a seated position. An additional bench or table is useful on which to place work awaiting attention, or in progress and between operations. Bench tops are ideally provided with a washable surface so that they can be kept clean. Work benches and tables should be shielded from direct strong sunlight. Electricity or gas points are needed for the heating of hot glues and finishing stoves.

The arrangement of benches, tables and equipment should be as logical as possible and so offer the best use of available light and space, together with convenience and comfort when working and moving about in the bindery.

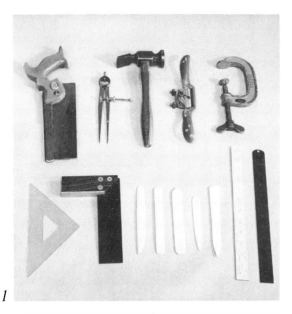

1

TOOLS AND EQUIPMENT

A significant amount of bookbinding can be achieved with relatively little plant. A small number of basic items are desirable and these can be added to as skills, needs or ambitions develop. A comprehensive range of tools and equipment for bookbinding is shown here and in appropriate places throughout this book.

1 Tenon-saw, dividers, backing-hammer, spoke-shave, G-clamp, set-square, carpenter's square, various bone-folders, boxwood ruler, steel ruler.

2

2 Oil stone, leather surfaced strop, pair of shears, pair of scissors, 'French' paring knife, 'German' paring knife, penknife, shoe-maker's knife, card-knife, steel straight-edge.

3 Paste-tub, glue-pot, polythene container for cold adhesives, a range of brushes, sponge.

4 *Back* nipping-press on wooden stand, *left* cutting-press (i.e. lying-press with runners for plough) together with plough and press-pin, *right* large lying-press, *front* small and large finishing or bench presses.

3

4

5

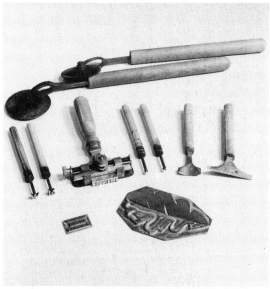

6

5 *Back left* pressing-boards, *back right* metal-edged pressing boards, *front* knocking-down iron, lead weights, cutting-boards metal-edged backing-boards, backing boards, smoothing-plane (for re-aligning backing and cutting boards).

6 Finishing tools: *back* fillet and roll, *centre* handle-letters, type-holder with type, decorative tools, gouge, pallet, *front* two blocks.

7 Sewing-frame, on which rest reels of tape and webbing together with thread in packet, unwrapped, in skein, and with skeins cut and plaited (Appendix 4). In the foreground is a bodkin, sewing-keys for use with tape, needles, sewing-keys for use with cord (shown here for comparison only), a ball of linen cord.

MATERIALS AND ADHESIVES

The following lists of materials and adhesives are likely to be of use in general bookbinding operations.

White or cream cartridge paper, white or cream bank paper, white newsprint, brown kraft paper, coloured Ingres paper, coloured Cobb paper, decorative printed and marbled papers, coloured cover papers.

Strawboard, millboard, chipboard.

Niger morocco goatskin, bookcloth and buckram woven covering-materials, white cotton label-cloth, mull (all shown in figure 8).

Fibre-felt (tough paper) covering-materials.

Scotch, flexible and case-making hot glues, polyvinyl-acetate (PVA) general purpose cold glue, wheat-flour paste (Appendix 5).

Gold leaf; gold, aluminium and pigment blocking foils.

Glaire (egg-albumen or resin-based mordant), gold rubber, vinegar, white Vaseline, cotton-wool, poster-colours, printing-inks.

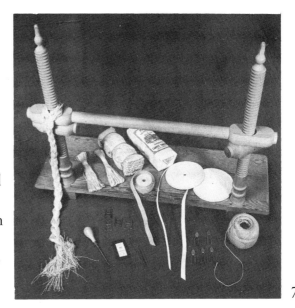

7

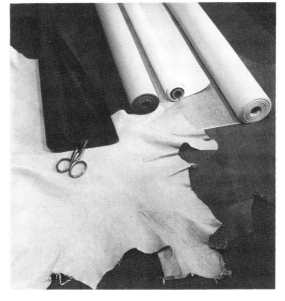

8

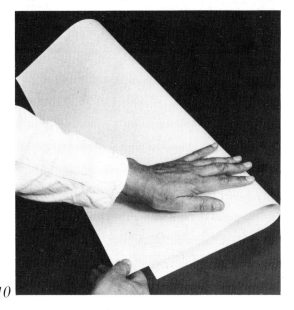

9

10

MACHINE DIRECTION in PAPER AND BOARDS

Most of the paper and boards used in bookbinding and book production is machine-made. It is a feature inherent in machine manufacture that the cellulose-fibres from which the paper or board is made tend to be drawn into one general direction. This general fibre direction is called the machine-direction or grain. Paper and board exhibit relatively less resistance when bent parallel with, rather than counter to, their machine-direction. When paper is made wet, as for example by the application of an adhesive, a predominant stretching or dimensional increase will occur at right angles to its machine-direction. Subsequently, shrinking back will take place as drying out proceeds. The unstable effects of such dimensional changes are controlled by a balanced or compensatory use of surface materials, particularly when mixed paper and board structures or other absorbent material laminations are envisaged.

In order to give greater ease in the opening of its leaves, greater rigidity and stability of its boards, elimination of creasing in endpaper paste-downs and elimination of the possibility of warping covers, the machine-direction in all the materials of a book should as a general rule run from head to tail. One exception may be made when preparing boards for oblong or landscape format books, but care must be taken when case-making and casing-in to keep the moisture content of the adhesives used to a minimum, thus avoiding excessive contrary shrinking of the various materials and consequent irregular warping of the covers.

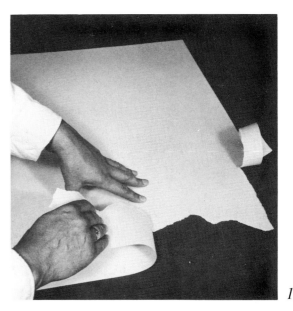

11

Testing for machine-direction

9-10 The bend test to determine machine-direction in paper. Paper bends more easily parallel with, rather than against, its machine-direction.

11 The tear test to determine machine-direction in paper. A relatively straighter tear is obtained with, rather than against, the machine-direction.

12 The wet test to determine machine-direction in paper. The strips of paper have been sponged with water. The direction along the tunnel of paper is indicative of its machine-direction.

12

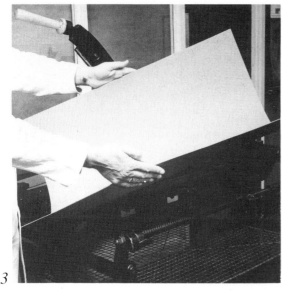

18

13

14

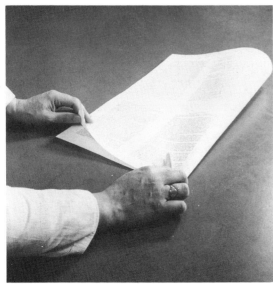

15

13 Bending a strawboard to determine its machine-direction.

THE MAKE-UP OF BOOKS AND FOLDING FROM SHEETS

Originally written before the introduction of metrication to printing and bookbinding, this chapter is retained in order to describe and record basic principles. The Quad Demy multiple most nearly equates to the international paper size A0, and A5 therefore may be compared with Demy Octavo (Appendix 1).

14 Most books begin their lives as flat printed sheets. The ultimate format of a book depends upon the size of the sheet and the way in which the printer has set out or imposed his pages of type-matter or illustration. Sheets are based on standard broadsheet sizes such as Crown, Demy, Royal (or their metric equivalents), or international paper sizes. For convenience and speed of printing, sheets may be larger than the broadsheet size, thus Double Crown or Quad Crown, etc, when they are termed multiples.

The basic unit of a book is called a section. Sections are formed when the printed sheet is subdivided by folding, or by cutting and folding, with due regard to the printed imposition and pagination (page numbering). Besides the subdivision of sheets into the common Crown Octavo or Demy Octavo section sizes, subdivisions can offer a widely varied section range using either long or short measure binding-edges to provide both upright (common) or oblong (landscape) format.

15-18 show the folding of a Demy broadsheet to Demy Octavo. The sheet is printed with eight pages on each side and will make a 16-page section. The sheet is positioned with its lowest page number facing downwards at the bottom left-hand corner. Using a bone-folder, three successive folds are then made, each fold halving a long edge. The second fold or bolt is slit with the bone-folder, in from its open end to just beyond centre (*17*), thus preventing creasing inside the section when the third and final fold is made. Note how the corner of the sheet is raised slightly so that the print on facing pages can be sighted accurately into position (folding to print).

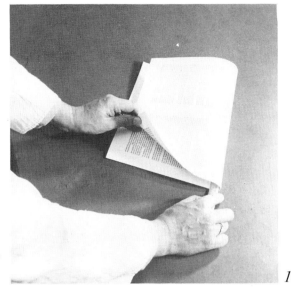

16

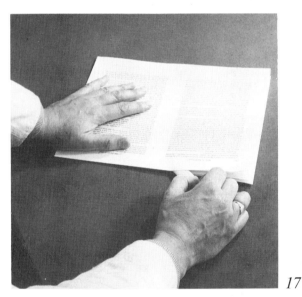

17

18

19

19　Most sheets are identified by an alphabetical or numerical signature-mark printed in sequence at the foot of the lowest numbered page (i.e. the first page) of each folded section. Alphabetical sequences normally adhere to tradition and use a twenty-three letter alphabet, omitting J, V and W. The half-title page is normally considered sufficient identification in itself for the first section. 2A or Aa indicates that there are more than twenty-three sections and that the alphabet is being used for a second sequence. B* would indicate that two sections are to be inserted one within the other, the outer section carrying the normal signature B. Signatures identify the sheet, help when positioning for folding, identify the folded section and help during the gathering of the sections into order. They can also help when checking section order for accuracy while collating (26).

Specifically a collating aid is the back-mark, printed to position on the back-folds of sections to form a series of steps, a break in which will indicate a misplaced section.

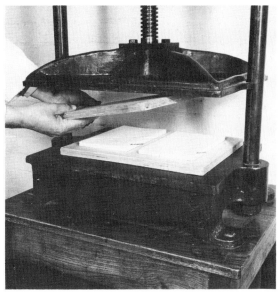

20

20　After folding, gathered sections are knocked-up to their heads and back-folds, and they are then placed between pressing-boards and into a nipping or standing-press to consolidate. Any tendency for the sections to slip can be avoided by reducing their numbers, perhaps by dividing a complete gathering into several parts.

21　A single-section case-binding. A multi-section case-binding. A quarter-leather library-style binding.

MULTI-SECTION CASE-BINDING

Proceeding with pressed sections as in figure *20* the following sequences demonstrate a multi-section case-binding. In case-binding the body of the book is built up separately from its cover or case. The two parts are joined together in a final operation called casing-in.

Preparing for Sewing

22   The pressed sections, with straw-board or chipboard on either side, have been knocked-up carefully to their head and back-edges and placed (head to the left) in a bench-press ready for marking-up. The book is Demy Octavo format made up of 18 sixteen-page sections.

23   Three ½ inch (13 mm) width tapes are positioned so that they divide the head to tail measurement into four equal parts.

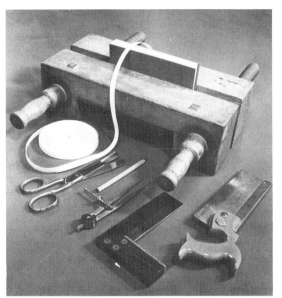

22

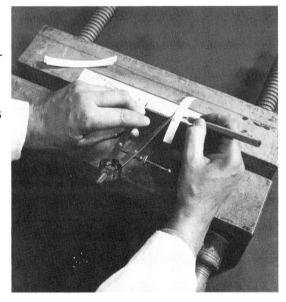

23

24

24 The tape positions are marked across the back-folds together with marks one tape-width in from head and tail for the kettlestitches (chain stitches linking section to section).

25 The kettlestitch marks are sawn-in to a depth of about $^1/_{16}$ inch ($1^1/_2$ mm) to accommodate the kettlestitches.

26 The sections are collated by checking the signatures for correct order immediately prior to sewing.

Sewing

27 The sewer is seated sideways to the bench. The three tapes shown ready are about 3 inches (75mm) longer than the

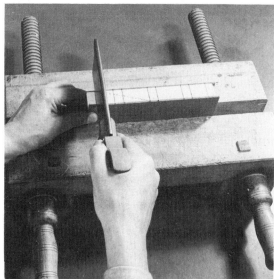

25

26

book is thick. The thread is 16-2 cord gauge (Appendix 4). The bookbinder's needle is Number 18.

28   The first section is faced down on the pressing-board and the tapes are placed to their marks with about one-third of their length tucked under the section. Sewing begins at the head kettlestitch position with the thread passing in and out of the back-fold and over the tapes in succession.

29   The needle is passed out from the first section and into the second section through the tail kettlestitch position. The left hand works inside the section in taking the needle, turning it round and pushing it out, whilst the right hand works similarly outside the section.

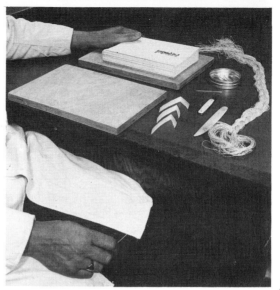

25

27

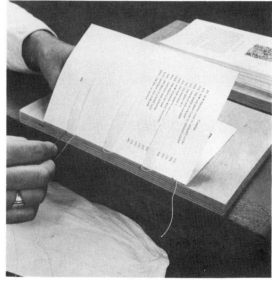

28

29

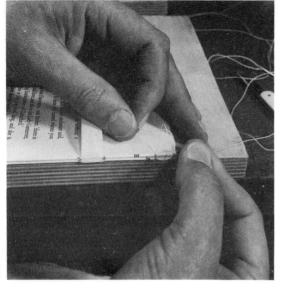

30

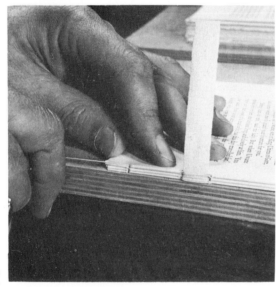

31

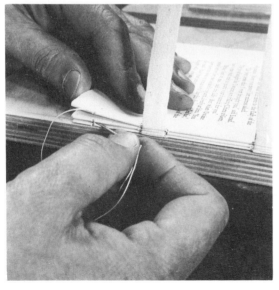

32

30   When the second section has been sewn the long and short ends of thread are drawn taut and tied together with a reef-knot, i.e. right over left and under, left over right and under.

31   The thread is drawn taut when the sewing of the third section is complete. To prevent tearing, draw threads taut in line with the back-folds of sections and not at right angles.

32-33   From the completion of the third section, kettlestitches can be worked at head and tail. To make a kettlestitch and thus tie down a section the needle is taken under the previous section sewn, out at the tail or head (whichever is the case) and up through the loop thus formed.

34 The sewing is tapped down with a bone-folder every few sections to keep it as firm as possible.

35 The head kettlestitch has been worked around the short end of thread left at the commencement of the sewing of the first section (*28* and *30*) and this end is now cut off after six sections have been sewn.

36 The needle can be conveniently

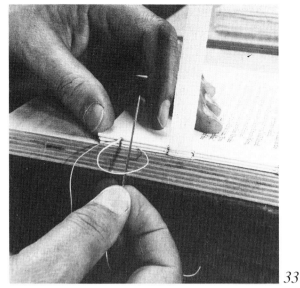

33

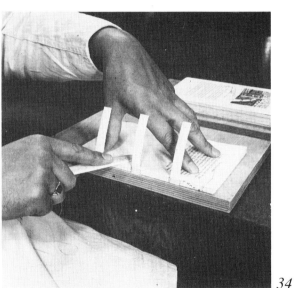

34

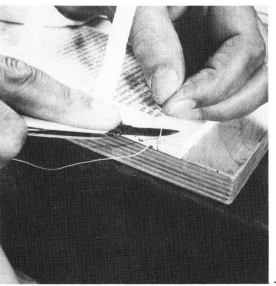

35

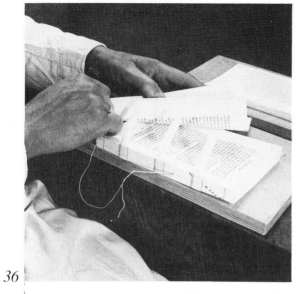

28

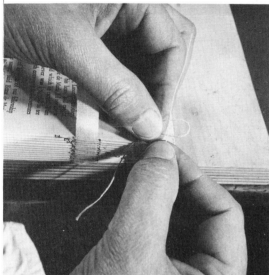

36

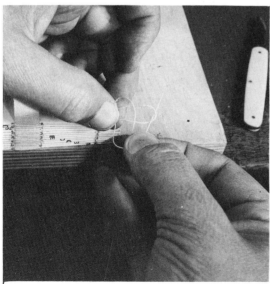

37

38

rested while both hands are occupied finding the centre of the next section.

37-38   A new thread is tied on using a sheet-bend. A loop is made in the old thread. The new thread does all the moving. It crosses the loop (37), goes round behind the loop, under itself, and then through the loop (38). The two ends of the old and the two ends of the new thread are drawn tight and the short ends of each are cut off close to the knot.

Knots should be arranged so that they can be pulled through the saw-cut of a kettlestitch position and rest in the fold of the section.

39 A double kettlestitch is made when the sewing is finished. The thread is then spiralled down the kettlestitches to a depth of six sections and cut off flush.

40 The needle holes are rubbed down with a bone-folder to prevent glue penetrating into the sections at a later stage.

39

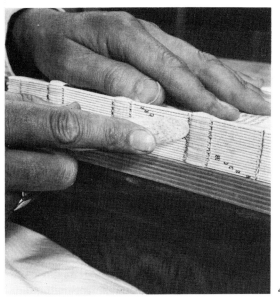

40

Swell

Sewing creates swell in what is now the back of the book. Swell helps to give the book shape at the rounding and backing stages (48-56). Swell is largely dependent upon the choice of sewing thread thickness in relation to the number and make-up of the sections. The amount of swell that should be aimed for to give the book a desired shape varies, depending upon the width or bulk of the body of the book and the height of the backing-joint required.

41 Using a knocking-down iron and hammer to reduce the swell until the back of the book is about one-quarter greater in bulk than its width at the foredge.

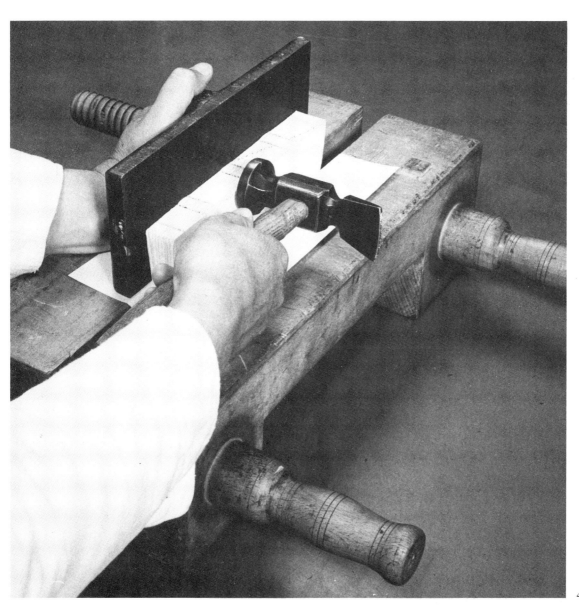

42

43

Endpapering

42 A pair of cartridge endpapers are cut and folded with head to tail machine-direction. The cartridge paper being used is of 120 g/m^2 substance.

43 ⅛ inch (3 mm) of the endpapers are exposed from under waste newspaper and their folds are pasted (Appendix 5). The endpapers are then pitched precisely level with the head and back-folds of the first and last sections of the book and rubbed down with the fingers. This type of attachment is called tipping-on.

44 The endpapered book is placed between boards and under a weight for a quarter of an hour.

Back-glueing

45 With pieces of strawboard on either side, the book is knocked-up carefully to its back and head and placed into a bench-press. The back is glued-up with thin, hot, flexible glue which is brushed thoroughly between the sections. After glueing, the book is removed from the press and put to one side, with its glued area just off a pressing-board. It should be dry and ready for cutting in half an hour.

44

45

46

Cutting

As little as possible should be removed from the leaves when cutting edges, particularly in the case of books being rebound. With new and uncut sections consideration should be given to the page layout and the planned proportion of its margins. An allowance is likely to be made for the removal of ⅛ inch (3 mm) from the shortest leaves of uncut sections. Before cutting any book, a check should be made for text or illustrations printed close to the edges and also the possible presence of any folded plates or maps. When using either a single-knife guillotine or a press and plough, edges are normally cut in the order of foredge, tail and head. A book is said to be 'trimmed' if the knife touches the longer leaves only and 'cut' if it touches every leaf.

46   A power-operated single-knife guillotine for cutting paper and book edges. Guillotines vary in detail but each

essentially consists of a bed on which the work rests, a back-gauge which determines the depth of cut, a clamp which holds the work firm, and a knife suspended from a carriage. The knife descends and makes a cut, and thence returns to its rest position. Qualified instruction should be obtained personally in the correct and safe operation of any guillotine available for use by a reader.

47   The head of this book has been cut in a guillotine. The book edge rests on a nylon cutting-stick set into the bed of the machine. Under the clamp and resting on top of the book is a fanned-out pad of paper preventing the swell in the back from becoming crushed and the book distorted. The knife has returned to its rest position leaving the off-cut of paper from the edge of the book in the foreground of the photograph. An alternative method of cutting book edges by the use of a cutting-press and plough is shown in figures *147-150*.

47

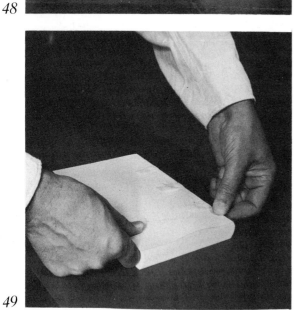

48

49

50

Rounding

48-49   Rounding the book to its traditional shape using hammer and fingers. In this operation the effect will be noted of the correct amount of swell left in the back after sewing. The round should be of an even arc. If the glue has become too set it should be softened by dampening with a moist sponge about five minutes before commencing to round the book.

Edge-colouring

50   The top-edge or head of the book may be coloured with poster colour mixed with diluted paste and applied with a pad of cotton-wool worked along the edge from back to foredge. After allowing a few minutes for drying, the book can be removed from between the waste strawboards and from under the weight (knocking-down iron).

Backing

51 The backing-height measure for case-binding is normally twice the thickness of the board to be used for the cover. This measure is marked from the fold of the endpapers at head and tail.

52 The backing-boards are adjusted to the backing-height mark.

53 The book, with backing-boards set, is lowered into a lying-press which is then screwed up as tightly as possible with its press-pin. Should the backing-boards slip whilst putting the book into the press it will be necessary to re-set them. Persistent slipping may be cured by dampening the inner face of the backing-boards. Lying-presses rest horizontally about 30 inches (75 cm) above floor-level on a stand called a press-tub.

54 In backing, the sections are knocked outwards with light glancing blows, using the face, and later the toe

51

52

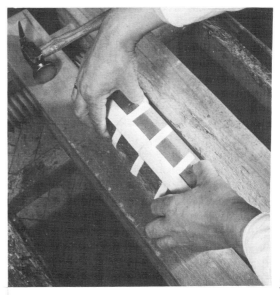

53

(55) of the backing-hammer. Roughly one-third of the sections are hammered to the left and one-third to the right, the centre third remaining virtually untouched by the hammer. On removal from the press the backing joints may be neatly sharpened against strawboards with a bone-folder (56).

Rounding and backing together deal with the problem of swell occasioned by sewing. Rounding distributes the swell over an arc. It produces a convex back which is aesthetically pleasing, together with a concave foredge eminently suited to opening. Backing fully distributes the swell. It helps to set and consolidate the round of the book. It provides defined joints from which the cover boards will hinge, and its bending outwards of the back-folds of the sections is an aid to flat opening of the leaves.

55

56

57

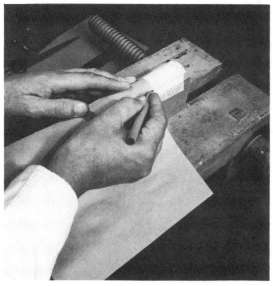

58

59

Back-lining

57-62 demonstrate back-lining. A first lining of mull and a second lining of kraft paper are used to give strength to the joints and back of the book.

57 The mull is cut to size 1 inch (25 mm) in width beyond each joint and $\frac{1}{8}$ inch (3 mm) short of the edges at head and tail. The back is brushed thoroughly with thin Scotch glue or a cold PVA adhesive worked carefully off the edges. The mull is positioned and rubbed down with a folder.

58 Kraft paper is measured to the exact width of the back of the book.

59 Two strips of the kraft paper are cut with head to tail machine-direction, each a little longer than the back of the book. One piece should be kept aside to act as a case-lining during case-making and it will be cut to the head to tail measure of the boards, when this is known. The strips are shown being cut with a penknife and a steel straight-edge on a piece of waste board.

60 The back is given a second glueing.

61 The kraft paper second lining is positioned and rubbed down.

62 The kraft paper is cut flush with head and tail.

60

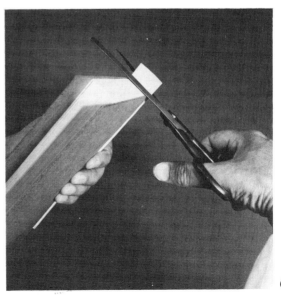

61

62

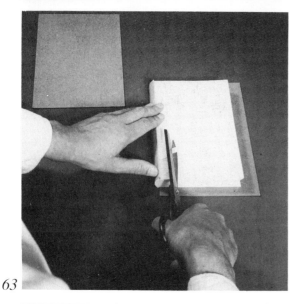

63

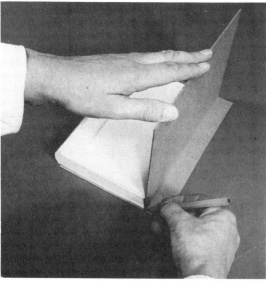

64

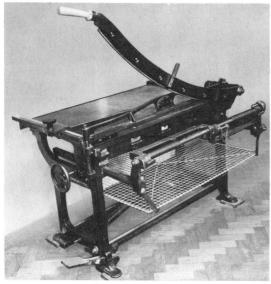

65

63 The slips of tape are trimmed level with the edge of the mull, thus completing the work on the body of the book.

Squaring boards

64 It will have been noted that from the completion of backing, the book has been kept continually between an oversize pair of strawboards to protect its joints. After cutting one long and one short edge to a right angle, the strawboards or chipboards are marked for size. With the good back-edge of board placed comfortably into the joint, the square (projection) of the board at head, tail and foredge, is judged equal to the board's own thickness. The board being used is 1400 g/m^2 (Appendix 2).

65-66 A board cutter. The example shown is a heavy-duty cutter, but this type of machine is available in smaller sizes. It consists of a bed, side-lay with rule, back-gauge, foot-operated clamp and two blades, one fixed and the other pivoted.

67   Boards can also be cut with a cutting-press and plough or with a small cutting-press and knife.

Cutting cover materials

68   Cutting the bookcloth covering material. Woven fabrics should normally be cut so that the joint of the book is parallel with the selvedge of the roll. There is greater resistance to opening if the warp threads (i.e. those running up the length of the roll) are allowed to cross the joints. The selvedge itself, being uneven, is cut off. Fibre-felt or paper covering materials should be cut with their machine-directions running from head to tail. The covering material is cut wider than the board edges to allow for a ⅝ inch (15 mm) turn-in all round.

66

67

68

Case-making

69   The bench laid out for case-making. At the back: pressing-boards,
weight, the book with boards set into the
joints but knocked flush with the edge
at the tail, a piece of kraft paper for rubbing-down, a pot of hot case-making
glue with large glue-brush. To the left:
the kraft paper case-lining, pencil,
shears, bone-folder. To the right: the
bookcloth covering material (with the
position of one board marked) lying face-
side downwards on a piece of waste newspaper.

46

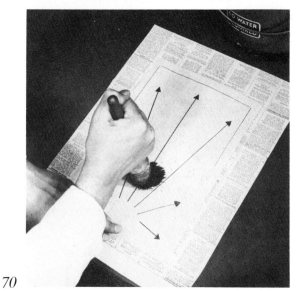

70

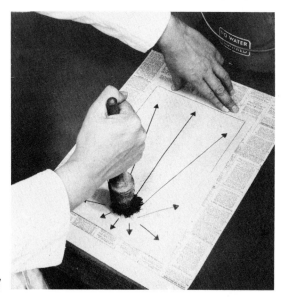

71

70-71 The case-making glue should be thin enough to run freely from the brush. The brush should be well charged and worked over the cloth as indicated by the arrows, using an even dabbing-out action rather than with dragged brush strokes. Alternative adhesives for this operation are a Scotch glue and paste mixture, or a PVA glue. The glued cloth is then transferred to the clear bench space shown in figure 63. The cloth is best lifted with middle fingers on the glued side and thumbs on the face side. The fingers should be wiped clean

72

immediately.

72   The book is positioned on the glued bookcloth.

73   The case-lining is positioned.

74   The book and boards are held firm and the cloth is drawn tightly around the back and then rubbed down with the palms on to the upper board.

75   The upper board (now attached to the cloth) is thrown back and marked as facing the endpaper paste-down leaf.

76   Using shears, the corners of the bookcloth are cut off at 45 degrees. The cut should be made at approximately one

73

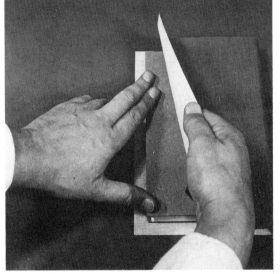

74

75

76

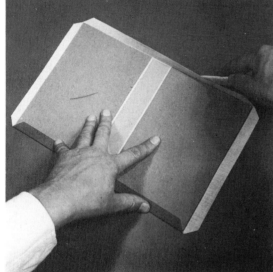

77

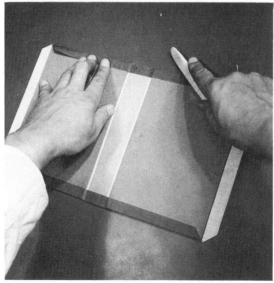

78

and a half times board thickness away from the corner of the strawboard.

77   Folding the turn-in tightly to the board edge. The head and tail turn-ins are worked first.

78   The head and tail turn-ins are pulled over the board edges as tightly as possible. A final rubbing-down is made with the bone-folder.

79   Using a finger-nail, or the sharpened point of a bone-folder, the small piece of cloth left at the board corners is nicked-down prior to the turning-in of

the foredge.

80 The face-side of the made case is rubbed down with a bone-folder. A piece of kraft paper acts as protection, preventing the covering material from becoming bruised from the rubbing action.

81 Checking the fit of the case around the body of the book. The spine of the case may be rubbed down flat through kraft paper after the check has been made and then the case placed between pressing boards and under a weight to dry out.

79

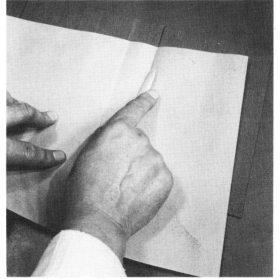

80

81

Tooling with foil

The use of foil for lettering is a comparatively simple process requiring no preliminary treatment of the covering material. Foil is composed of gold, aluminium or pigment, sandwiched between a carrier film (such as Melinex) on its upper side and a heat-sensitive adhesive on the side placed to the work. Lettering or decoration is effected by impressing a heated metal die (either in the form of a hand-tool or a block) on to the upper side of the foil. This activates the adhesive and a gold or coloured impression of the die used is left in the covering material.

83

82 A bench laid out for lettering. Included in the layout is a pad of paper on which titling arrangements may be written, a set of handle-letters placed in alphabetical order around the finishing stove, a pad of wet cotton-wool in a saucer for cooling, and a further pad of dry cotton-wool for cleaning off. (It should be noted that for convenience in photographing these lettering sequences the stove was moved from its normal permanent position on a fixed heat-proof base.)

83 A handle-letter on the finishing stove, showing the nick cut across its shank to indicate the top of the letter.

84

84 Using the cooling-pad of wet cotton-wool. If the tool does not sizzle it is too cool. When the tool does sizzle it should be kept on the pad until the sizzle stops, when it is ready for use.

85 Impressing a handle-letter through Whiley's ZRO gold foil held to the spine of the case by transparent adhesive tape. The foil has been marked-up on its surface with guide-line and ticks made with a point of the dividers. The tops of the letters touch the guide-line. The ticks are spaced equally along the guide-line but the centre of letters may require placing slightly to the left or right of their tick depending upon their particular width and shape, so that the spaces left between letters appear to be optically even. Pressure required will vary depending upon the size of the face, but should be just enough in order to obtain a good impression into the particular covering material used. Large sized letters and decorative tools will require a slight rocking of the handle in order to get the impression solid all over. If the tools used are too cool, the gold or colour will be incomplete, or entirely absent. If the tools are too hot the gold or colour may fill-in or it may extend beyond the actual face area. In the latter event the impression can be cleared using the dampened point of a sharpened match-stick. Incomplete impressions can be made good by covering the particular area with foil and re-tooling. The finished work may be rubbed off with dry cotton-wool to remove any flecks of gold or pigment from the cover surface.

Whilst tooling is the manual application of heated metal dies to the cover surface, blocking is their mechanical application. The dies used for mechanically applied impressions are called blocks. Blocking is used when the size of die required is too large for manual application or when the quantity of work being produced is numerous and repetitive. Blocks are supplied by a commercial block-maker from art-work provided by the binder. Copper or zinc are commonly used for the manufacture of blocks.

85

86

87

Blocking with foil

86   shows two copper blocks glued to the heat-plate of a hand-operated electrically heated blocking-press.

87   shows a blocked case ready for removal from the sliding bed of the press. The heat-plate and blocks are in position under the heat-box. The gold foil is fed downwards from its reels and between the blocks and the case to the back of the machine.

Blocking can also be carried out by the use of brass type locked into a chase attached to the heat-plate.

Casing-in and pressing

88 The finished case is pulled gently up and down over the edge of the bench to round its spine.

89 Waste newspaper under the endpaper paste-down leaf protects the book edges during casing-in. The slips of tape and the mull are pasted but an excessive amount of adhesive in the joint should be avoided as it will squeeze out under pressure.

88

89

90

91

92

90-92 The waste paper is removed and the case is closed on to the paste-down leaves, the squares are adjusted if necessary (by sliding the body) and the book is placed between boards and into the press. The press used is the nipping-press shown in figure 4. A larger press for flat pressing is known as a standing-press but the one illustrated is more than adequate for this operation. The book is slightly forward from centre to reduce pressure on the joints. Pressure should be reasonably firm at first but may be reduced after about an hour. It is ideal if books can remain in the press overnight.

Opening

93　On removal from the press the boards are opened and the endpaper fly-leaf is folded back to its paste line.

94　Opening of the body of the book should be done by taking a few leaves from the front and the rear of the book simultaneously, and gradually working towards its centre, thus easing the back-linings.

The case-bound book is now completed and ready for use.

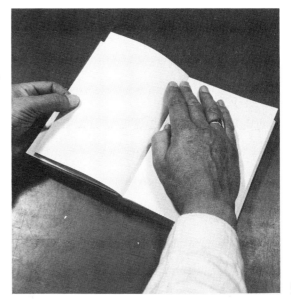

93

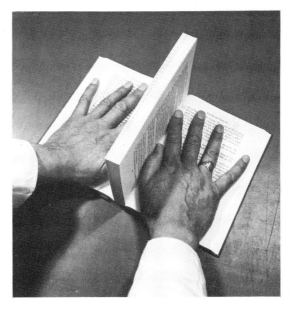

94

Pre-printed and blocked cases

95-98   A group of case-bound books
produced by students of Oxford
Polytechnic. In some examples the
bookcloth was pre-printed by offset-
lithography before being made up into a
case. The cases were then blocked in gold
or pigment foil. These bindings had too
few sections to warrant rounding and
backing. They were therefore left square-
back with the boards set $\frac{1}{4}$ inch (6 mm)
from the fold of the endpapers.

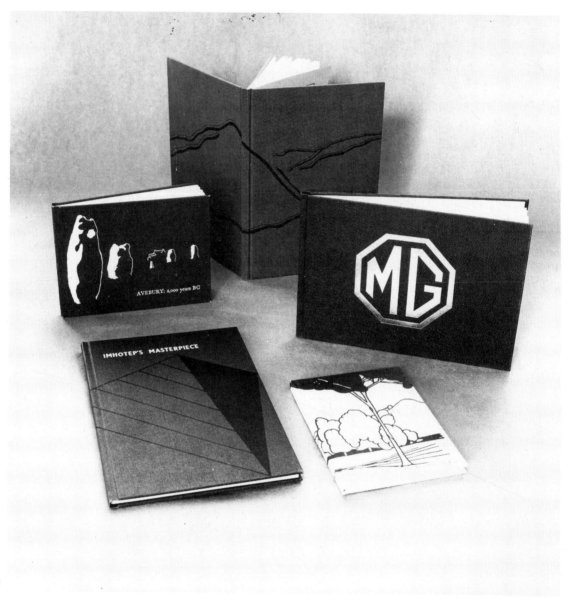

MAKING DECORATED PAPER

99-105   show simple methods for making decorative papers which may then be effectively used as endpapers or as board siding papers.

Paste papers

99   Paste, coloured with poster paint, is applied to cartridge paper.
100-101   Combs cut from millboard are used to make formal or free patterns, as desired.

99

100

101

102

102 Dryad printing sticks being used to impress patterns into the paste. Interesting results can also be obtained by rolling the sticks across the paper. In effect, anything that will activate the brushed paste can be used. The papers
need to be kept between boards when dry.

Relief printing

103 Torn and cut pieces of mull being placed on a glued millboard to produce a relief printing surface. Other materials such as teased-out string, sacking, glass paper, corrugated paper, leaves, feathers, etc. may be used.

104 The relief surface is rolled with printing ink.

105 Cartridge paper is placed on the inked surface, rubbed down by hand, and then carefully removed. Superimposed prints can be made using the same or other coloured inks and from the same or alternative reliefs.

Coloured paper can be used successfully for both types of decorated papers.

103

104

105

CASE-BINDING VARIANTS

The case made in figures *68-81* is in full cloth. It could have been made in a fibre felt or other strong paper.

106   shows some variations in case-making using cloth and decorative papers.

Back left   quarter cloth with paper sides.

Back centre   quarter cloth with paper sides turned-in on the back-edge.

Back right   paper case with head and tail cloth strip.

Front left   half cloth with paper sides.

Front right   half cloth with paper sides and cloth foredge strip.

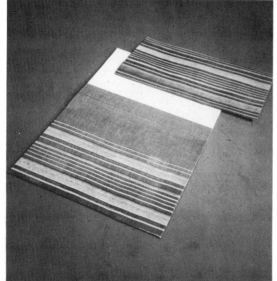

107

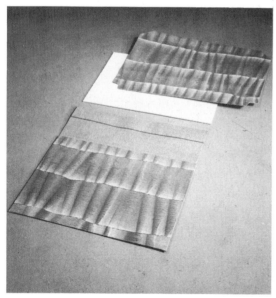

108

107 Quarter cloth with paper sides. The spine strip normally overlaps the board by between one quarter and one fifth of the board width. A narrower overlap can look effective provided its width is compatible with strength. The cloth spine is turned-in at head and tail over the board edges and case lining. A paper side normally overlaps the cloth by $\frac{1}{8}$ inch (3 mm). Its corners are treated as in figure 76.

108 Quarter cloth with paper sides turned-in on the back-edge. The case-lining is glued to the cloth spine, the head and tail turn-ins of which are glued and rubbed down. A pencil line is made on the cloth to mark the board position. The paper side, which may conveniently have its corners pre-cut as indicated, is glued to the board and only its back-edge is turned-in. The cloth is glued up to the pencil line, to receive the board, which is then pitched to position. The head, tail and finally the foredge of the paper side are then turned-in. A quick nip in the press between pressing-boards protected with plain white newsprint ensures good adhesion of the boards.

109   Half cloth with paper sides. The pencil line marked for the position of the cloth corner is measured at 45 degrees in from the corner of the board and should traditionally correspond to the amount by which the spine strip overlaps the board.

110   Half cloth with paper sides and cloth foredge strips. The proportion of the different components can be varied at will.

109

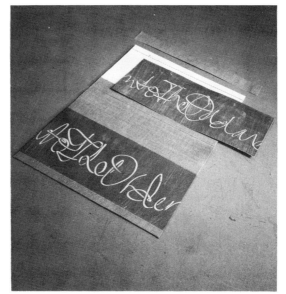

110

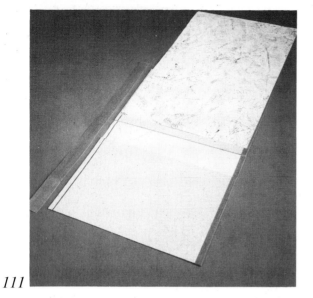

111

112

113

111 Paper case with head and tail cloth strips. The paper spine strip (without turn-in) overlaps the inside of the boards by about ¾ inch (20 mm) and reinforces the paper cover. The head and tail strips show most effectively if they appear narrow on the face side. The paper cover is turned-in on its foredge only. Decorative paste-papers are unsuitable for this style as they are liable to crack at the joints.

SINGLE-SECTION CASE-BINDING

112 Two 4-page cartridge endpapers are cut, folded and outset around a single-section book. A piece of mull is cut to reinforce the back-fold.

113 A paring-stone (lithographic stone, marble or plate-glass surface) is glued out with thin Scotch or PVA adhesive. The mull is placed on the glued surface and rubbed down through waste newspaper. It is then lifted and drawn around the endpapered section using a fold of kraft paper.

114 A bodkin is used to pierce three holes through the back-fold, in the centre and 1 inch (25 mm) from head and tail.

115 The thread passes out through the centre hole, in at the head and down the fold, out at the tail and back through the centre, where the ends are tied with a reef knot across the long stitch.

116 Boards for this style are cut with normal squares but their back-edges are set ¼ inch (6 mm) from the back-fold of the book. Cases are made without a case lining.

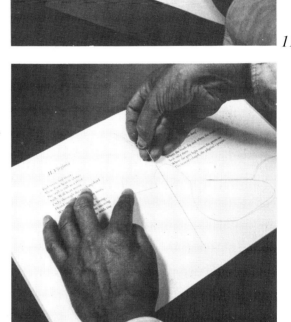

114

115

116

117

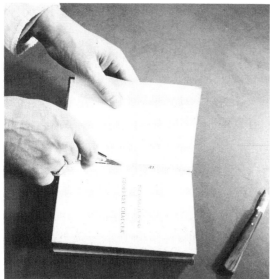

118

119

PREPARING A BOOK FOR RE-BINDING

Dissecting

117 An old case-binding is to be re-bound in a quarter-leather library-style binding. A penknife is stropped before use.

118 The endpaper fly-leaf is pulled back and the book is cut from its case by slitting through the mull.

119 Loose back-linings are removed.
120-121 Threads are cut at the centre of sections which are then pulled firmly away from the body of the book.
122-123 Glue fragments are cleaned from the back-folds.
124 The old backing grooves are gently hammered-out on the knocking-down iron, after the grooves have been bent by finger pressure in reverse direction over the edge of a pressing board.

120

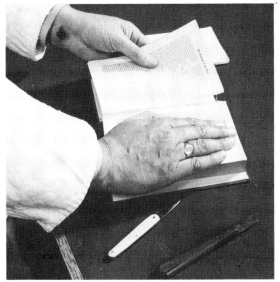

121

122

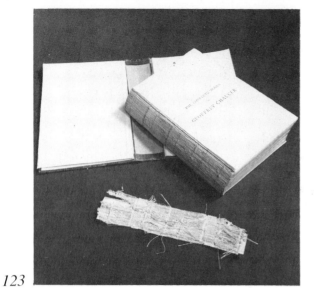

123

124

125

Guarding

125   Guards for repairing the weakened back-folds of sections are marked out on a sheet of bank, mould-made, or other suitable repairing paper, substance approximately 45 g/m^2.

126   A knife and straight-edge are used to cut the guards. Guards should be cut long grain and approximately 10 mm in width.

127   Paste is off-set on to the guards from the surface of a paring-stone. Up to four guards at a time are rubbed down through paper.

128-130 The pasted guards are taken from the stone and drawn around the back of sections.

Guarding should be adequate to ensure a strong book. Discretion should be exercised in the guarding of books containing numerous thin sections, where over guarding may create a problem of undue swell. In such instances it may be judged wise to guard the first few and the last few sections of the book, and then only the very weak or badly torn sections.

126

127

128

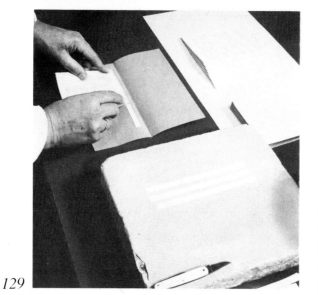

129

Attaching plates

131-133   A single-leaf plate is pasted ⅛ inch (3 mm) along the back-edge of its reverse side. A guard is attached to the pasted edge and the plate is allowed to dry-out between boards. The guard is then folded and hooked around a section, from which it will hinge freely after sewing.

134   For a library-style binding, ½ inch (12 mm) width tapes cut from cotton label-cloth have been attached with paste to the first and last sections. Two-

130

131

thirds of the width of each tape have been brought around the section but left unpasted at this stage, being tipped to a cloth-jointed endpaper after sewing (*148*). Guarded and taped sections should be allowed to dry thoroughly before pressing (*20*).

QUARTER-LEATHER LIBRARY-STYLE BINDING

The library-style binding to be demonstrated will have its boards attached before covering and so offer a

77

132

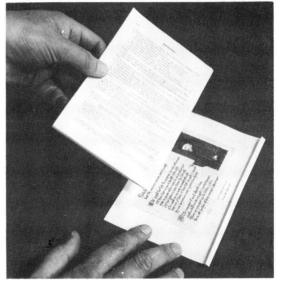

133

134

135

136

137

contrast in construction with that of the case-binding.

Cloth-jointed endpapers

135   A cloth-jointed endpaper requires one 1 inch (25 mm) width strip of good quality bookcloth, two 4-page folds of white cartridge paper and two single leaves of coloured Cobb paper or other suitable coloured or decorated paper. These materials should be doubled to make a pair of endpapers.

136   The cloth joints are glued out

with a Scotch glue and paste mixture, or a PVA glue (either are suitable for making this endpaper). One fold of cartridge paper is pitched to cover two-thirds of the width of the cloth and the other pitched to cover the remaining one-third. There should be a $^1/_{16}$ inch (1$^1/_2$ mm) gap between the folds.

137-139 The single leaves of Cobb paper (cut so that they overlap the cloth by $^1/_8$ inch (3 mm) are glued-out and lined-in. A piece of white card (called a fence) prevents the linings from sticking together when the endpapers are given a

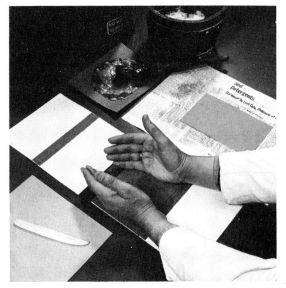

138

139

140

141

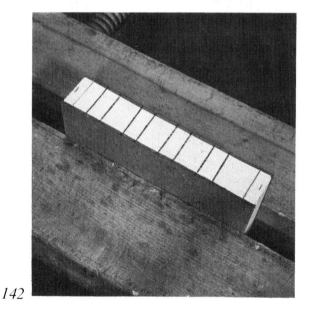

142

light quick nip in the press. After being removed from the press the endpapers should be allowed to dry thoroughly between boards and under a weight.

140 The endpapers, positioned with the two-thirds width of cloth away from the book, provide a waste leaf, a pastedown leaf, a coloured lined fly-leaf, and a white fly-leaf.

Marking-up for sewing

141-142 The Crown Octavo book is to be sewn on four ⅜ inch (9 mm) width tapes. Marks are made ⅛ inch (3 mm) from head and tail (to indicate an optimum measure for eventual edge cutting) and between these the back is divided into five equal parts. The tape width position is marked to the head side of each one-fifth division. (After covering in leather this will provide a tail panel of greater depth than the remaining panels.) Saw-cuts for the kettlestitches are made ⅜ inch (9 mm) from head and tail. The endpapers should not be sawn-in.

Sewing on a frame

A sewing-frame can be used to provide greater control when sewing a thick book, or for convenience when sewing several books marked-up with identical tape positions. Sewing-keys hold firm the lower end of tapes which are passed

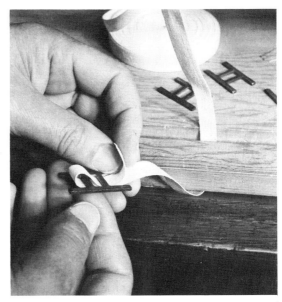

143

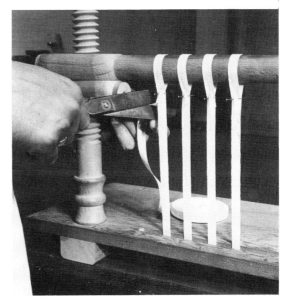

144

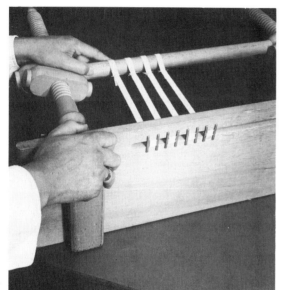

145

146

through the slot in the frame and pinned over the cross-bar.

143-147 show the setting up and use of a sewing-frame. The actual sewing process is as described for case-binding, with the exception that the endpapers are sewn through their cloth-joints as though they were sections. If several books are sewn on the frame at one time, each should be sewn independently of the next. When the sewing of a stack of books is completed, their tapes may be slid through the sewing and cut off to give slips of suitable length. Allowance should be made for this when setting up the tapes on the frame.

After sewing, the needle holes are rubbed down and the swell is reduced as in figures *40-41*.

148 The cotton reinforcement strips (*134*) are pasted and the endpapers are carefully positioned on to them. The book is then placed between boards and under a weight for a quarter of an hour (*44*). It is then glued-up as in figure *45*.

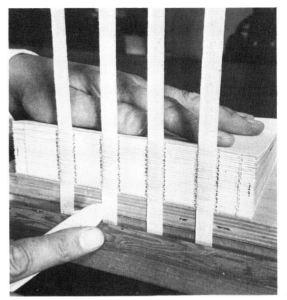

147

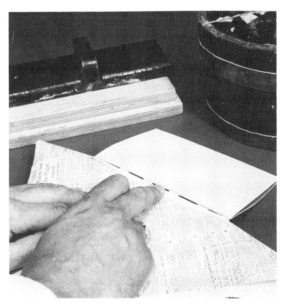

148

149

Split-boards

149   A strawboard of 1400 g/m^2 is glued to a millboard 1 mm in thickness (Appendix 2) with PVA glue or a mixture of Scotch glue and paste. The strawboard is shown covering about 1½ inches (38 mm) of the width of the millboard while the latter is being glued-out. The strawboard is then turned over head to tail and placed down on the millboard, the unglued portion of which will form the split. Made split-boards should be pressed overnight.

Cutting with press and plough

150   The cutting edge of a plough knife.

151   At top left a plough is standing on end showing its knife in position. The runners for the plough are seen screwed to the top of a lying-press thus converting it into a cutting-press. The book has

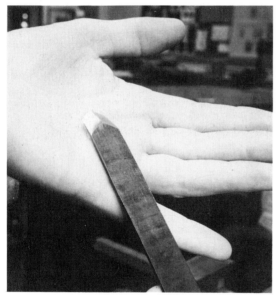

150

been tied with tape to keep it square. The amount to be cut off the foredge has been measured from the endpaper back-fold and marked on the waste leaf. A cutting-board is being placed to this mark and when in the press will be flush with the top of the right-hand cheek. The cutting-board on which the book rests is protected by a piece of millboard and will remain slightly above the edge to act as a 'cut against'.

151

152 As the plough is worked forwards and backwards its screw is turned slowly, advancing the knife which gradually cuts across the book edge.

153 To avoid problems of swell, the book should be rounded and backed before getting it into the press to cut head and tail. A backing height of one and a half times the thickness of the made split-boards is normal for this style. The head as shown has been cut, and the off-cut clinging to the sections at the turn of the backing is being removed with a sharp knife.

152

153

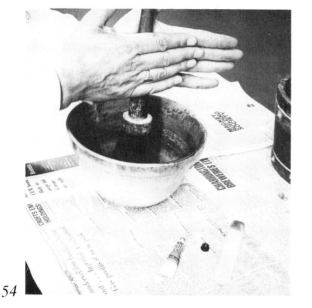

154

155

Sprinkling

154-155   Sprinkling is a common form of edge treatment for library bindings. Poster colour mixed with paste and thinned with water is prepared in a basin. An unbridled glue-brush is dipped into the colour and twirled between the hands until the bristles are almost dry. The brush is beaten against a press-pin held a few inches from the book and fine spots of colour are transferred to its edges. It should be noted that the quality of the sprinkle has been tested on the waste newsprint prior to working it directly on the edge.

Setting the back and attaching boards

156 The waste-leaves of the endpapers are glued-out and folded back into the joints, sandwiching the slips of tape and forming a tongue. The book is pressed with boards protected by plain newsprint.

157 Whilst in the press the back is pasted and allowed to soak for a few minutes. Surplus adhesive is scraped

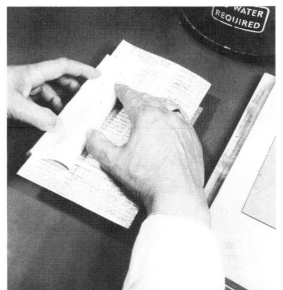

156

157

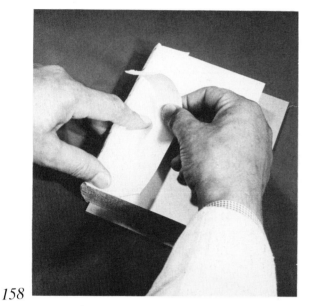

158

159

from the back with a piece of board. The back is then wiped clean with a damp sponge. The book should remain in the press until it is dry. This operation sets the shape of the book.

158 On removal from the press the folded waste-leaves are torn with a feathered edge about 1 inch (25 mm) away from and parallel with the joints. The tongue which remains is shortened at head and tail by 1 inch (25 mm). This tongue will provide the means by which the split-boards are attached to the body of the book.

159   When cutting split-boards to size
the normal squares are given, but there
should be a gap allowed between the
back-edges and the backing-joints equal
to twice the board thickness. This will
provide freedom in opening and produce
what is known as a french joint.
160   The split-board is opened and
glued.
161   The boards are positioned (thinner
board to the book), the squares are set
and the book is placed into a nipping or
standing press overnight.

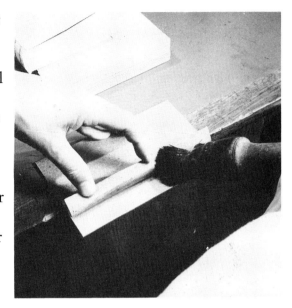

160

161

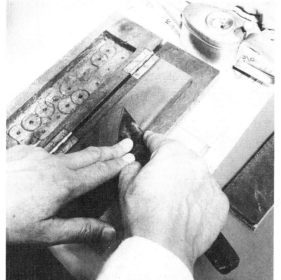

162

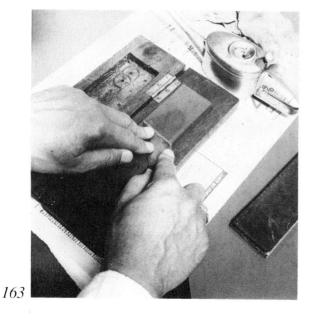

163

Knife-sharpening

162-165 show the sharpening of a 'German' paring-knife. The knife is bevelled on one edge and flat on the other.

162 The bevelled edge is placed to the oil-stone and worked up and down the stone until a burr can be felt on the flat edge of the blade.

163 The knife is now reversed and the burr is removed by carefully drawing the flat edge of the blade down the stone.

164   Bevelled and flat edges are alternatively stropped to remove any fragments of metal and to produce a keen cutting edge. A strop can be made by mounting a piece of hide and a piece of fine emery cloth on opposite sides of thick board.

165   The point of the knife is rounded-off on the side of the oil-stone in order to prevent it damaging the leather when paring.

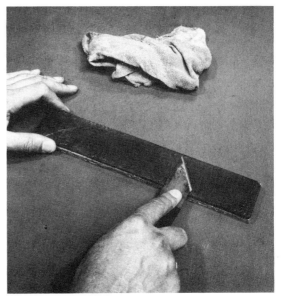

164

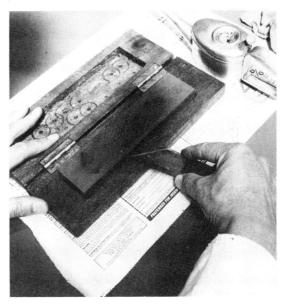

165

166

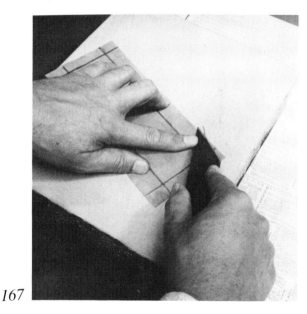

167

Leather

A good quality leather remains one of the best materials for covering. Leather can be strong yet supple, pleasant to work, and satisfying to look at and handle. Calf, sheepskin and pigskin are all used for bookbinding purposes but the most popular covering leather among craft-bookbinders is a sumac-tanned, aniline-dyed, Niger morocco type goatskin, acid-free and resistant to atmospheric pollution (Appendix 3).

166 A paper template is used as a guide when cutting leather for the library binding. This should be large enough to overlap the boards by 1 inch (25 mm) and provide a ¾ inch (20 mm) turn-in at head and tail.

Paring leather

The purpose of paring is to systematically reduce the thickness of leather so that it will function properly, be more easily worked and at the same time provide an acceptable measure of neatness to the finished book. Paring must be a planned operation, as any reduction in the thickness of leather is a reduction in its strength.

Old lithographic stones, or marbled slabs, make very suitable paring-stones. 167 shows the line of the joints and the turn-in marked on the underside of the leather with a soft pencil. Edge-paring begins with a back stroke.

168 Making a forward stroke. Movements should be as even as possible. The

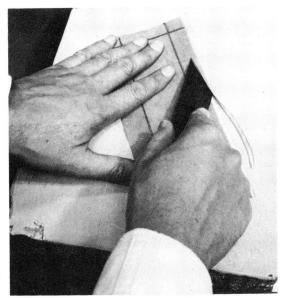

168

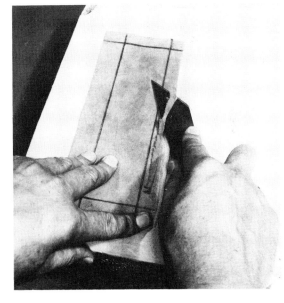

169

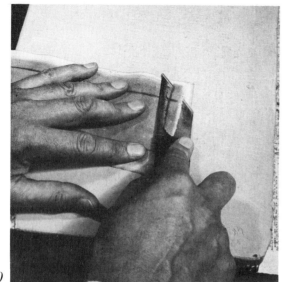

170

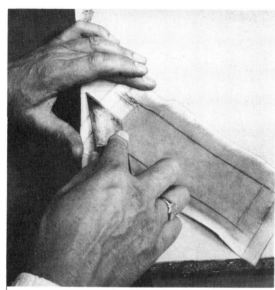

171

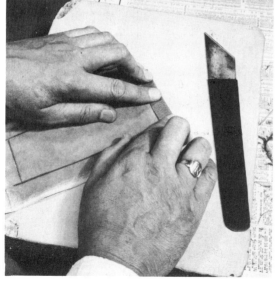

172

knife must be sharp and must not saw at the leather. The more the handle is tilted up the greater is the danger of cutting through the leather.

169 The knife being used almost flat to remove the ridge from preliminary edging strokes.

170 The knife being used almost flat to extend the paring at head and tail to a point just beyond the turn-in mark.

171 Using the heel of the knife to fluff away the leather between the lines of the joints and to the depth of the turn-in so that the latter will not protrude. The turn-in line will require re-marking on the leather together with a further line to control the extent of this paring.

172　Fingers feel and check the progress of the paring.

173　The heel of the knife may be used to pare along the line of the joints if it is considered that the thickness of the leather will preclude the free opening of the book.

174　A spokeshave being used (after edge-paring) to thin down an over-thick piece of leather which is protected with a backing-board while being held to the stone with a G-clamp.

175　Using a 'French' paring knife for the same operation as shown in figure 171.

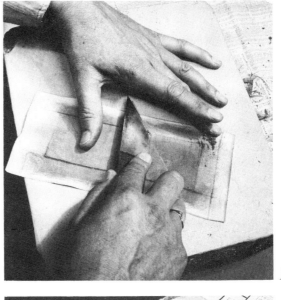

173

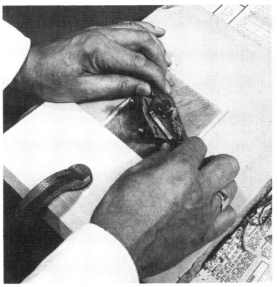

174

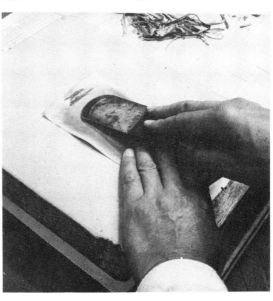

175

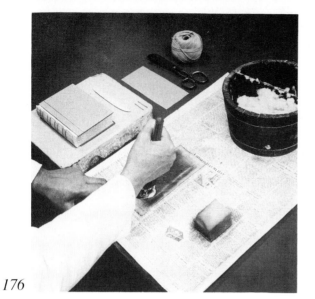

176

Covering

176 The leather is dampened with water on its face-side, turned over and pasted-out. After a few minutes' soaking, it is re-pasted. The paring-stone will act as a working surface and should be sponged clean as necessary. On the corner of the stone rest two paste-soaked pieces of hemp or linen cord cut to the width of the back and ready for insertion into the turn-in where later they will help form a head-cap. The back of the book is pasted.

177 The leather is drawn round the back and pressed down with a bone-folder into the space left between board and backing, thus forming the french joint.

177

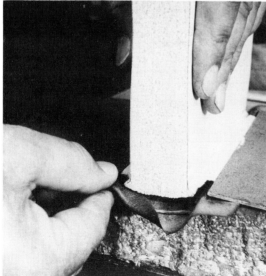

178

178   A piece of the pasted hemp is introduced at each turn-in so that eventually it will sit neatly on the edge of the book. The turn-in (which is pasted where it will touch the back of the book), is then brought over the edge of the boards, and tucked down the back, leather to leather.

179   The turn-in is smoothed to the boards and any surplus of leather worked to the back-edges.

180   The spine is rubbed down through kraft paper.

181   The book is tied around its joints with linen or hemp cord.

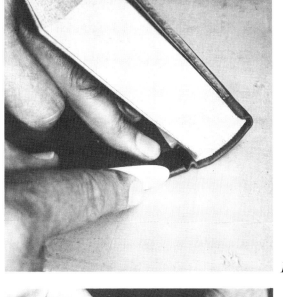

179

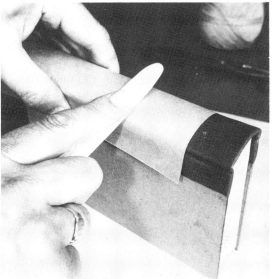

180

181

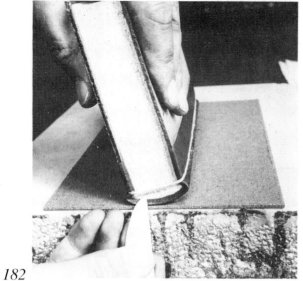

182

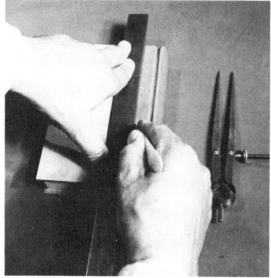

183

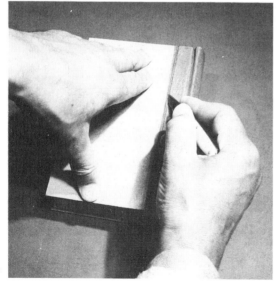

184

182 The head-cap is smoothed and shaped at 45 degrees to the head and tail edges.

The leather is finally sponged over and the book placed for safety between cartridge paper and pressing-boards until the next day, when the cord can be removed, the leather dampened at the joint and the boards opened.

183-185 Trimming-out the edge of the leather will ensure a neat fit of the cloth side.

183 A folder mark is made about ⅛

inch (3 mm) in from the edge of the leather, parallel with and an equal amount in from the back-edge of both boards.

184 A small strip is removed from the edge of the leather with a bevelled cut made along the folder mark.

185 Cloth sides are cut, glued and pitched up the bevel and into the folder mark.

186-187 The cloth sides are turned-in with a 'library-corner'.

185

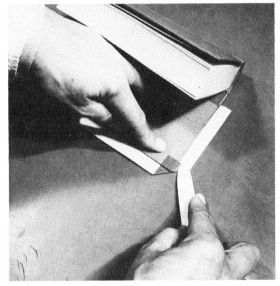

186

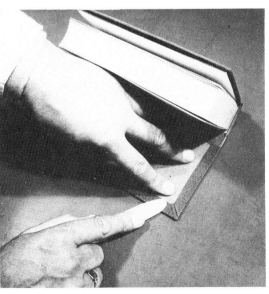

187

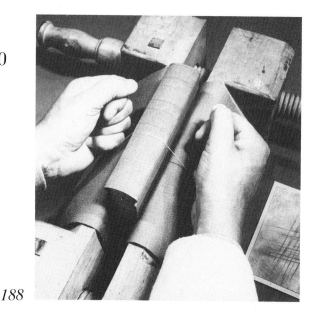

188

FINISHING
Blind tooling

This is the application of finishing-tools to a book cover with impression only, and without the use of gold or colour.
188 The spine of the quarter-leather library-style binding is divided out into shallow bands and panels. The bands relate to the positions of the tapes on which the book was sewn, and their widths should be checked for accuracy, together with those of the panels. A tick made on the surface of the leather with the point of the dividers will provide a suitable mark for aligning the piece of thread, which is then drawn left and right across the spine.
189 The friction mark left by the thread acts as a guide when a single-line

pallet is worked in blind over the spine. The pallet should be heated and cooled in the way shown for a handle-letter in figures *82-84*. If desired, dark impressions can be produced if the leather is dampened slightly and re-worked with a cool tool. Alternatively a pallet line can be polished-in by cooling down the tool and working it backwards and forwards across its original impression.

190   A single-line fillet is worked along the leather where it touches the cloth. If over-heated on the finishing-stove a fillet will require cooling under a cold tap. If the wheel is wedged with a small piece of wood it may also be used to polish-in an impressed line. Rolls are similar to fillets in general appearance but their edges are cut with a decorative face.

189

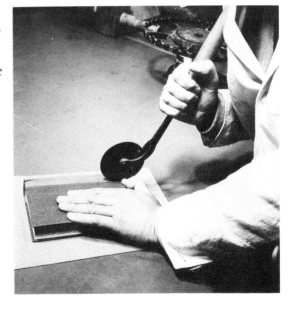

190

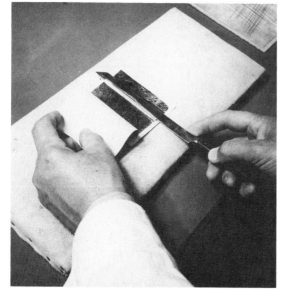

191

192

Direct-lettering with gold leaf and type

Glaire is an albuminous mordant used when tooling with gold leaf. It is applied wet to a book cover and allowed to dry. Gold leaf is given a temporary attachment to the glaired surface by applying a little white Vaseline to the latter. The glaire congeals under the application of the finishing-tools and thus the gold impression is made. The making of glaire is described in Appendix 6. The Niger morocco library-style binding will require its panel prepared for lettering. It should be sponged with a 50 per cent dilution of vinegar in water and when this is dry, one coat of glaire. When the glaire is dry the panel is lightly greased with white Vaseline applied with a small pad of cotton-wool. *191-192* A leaf of gold is removed from its book and placed on the calf-suede covered gold cushion. It is gently breathed on to make it lie flat, before being cut into convenient sizes with the narrow-bladed gold knife. (A light dressing of bath-brick dust or powdered pumice spread on the cushion with the gold knife will keep both cushion and knife clean and will facilitate the cutting of the gold leaf).

193 A pad of cotton-wool, first drawn across the hair, is used to lift the gold leaf from its cushion and then to press it down on to the panel. A second thickness of gold may be used with advantage provided the first thickness is breathed on before the second is padded down.

194 A piece of thread lightly drawn across the gold will provide a guide-line. An impression of the type on a strip of paper indicates the length to be accommodated so that its beginning can be ticked in the gold.

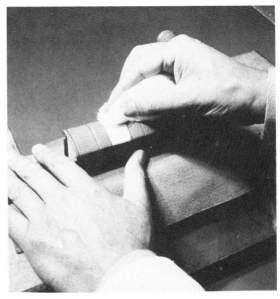

193

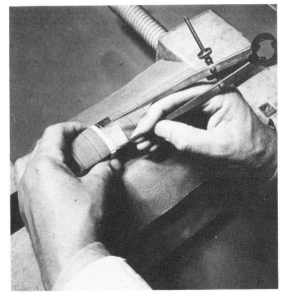

194

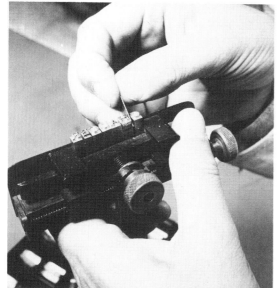

195

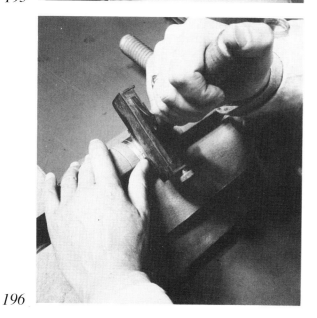

196

195   The line of brass type is being 'letter-spaced' in a type-holder.

196   The type-holder is heated on the finishing stove, cooled in the normal way and impressed across the gold.

197   After the type is impressed the surplus gold is removed with a specially prepared gold rubber or soft India rubber.

Direct lettering with gold leaf can be carried out on a cloth case-binding. The book to be lettered is first cased-in. The vinegar-water wash is omitted. One coat of glaire is applied.

Lettering in gold leaf with handle-letters and a paper pattern

The lettering is impressed into bank paper cut to the size of the panel. A pencilled guide-line and divider ticks aid in positioning the letters.

198 The paper pattern is fixed to the spine of the book with transparent adhesive tape and blind tooling is carried out through the impressions in the pattern. The pattern is removed from the spine which is then re-tooled in blind, directly into the leather, to sharpen the impressions obtained through paper.

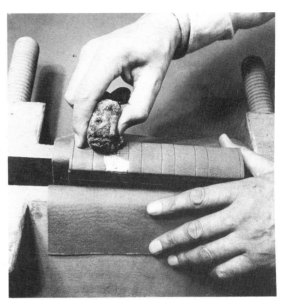

197

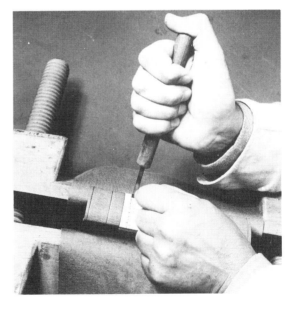

198

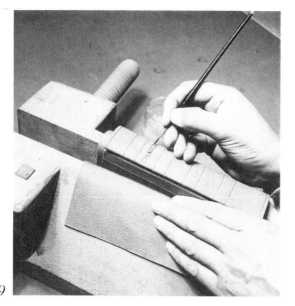

199

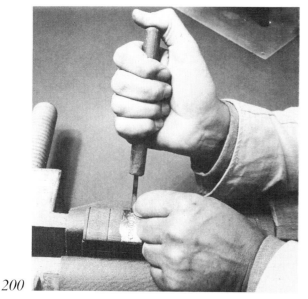

200

199 The panel is sponged with vinegar-water and then two coats of glaire are applied to the blind impressions with a fine pointed water-colour brush (an operation commonly known as 'pencilling-in').

When the glaire is dry the panel is greased and at least two layers of gold leaf are padded into the impressions, to ensure that they are completely covered.

200 The final tooling is carried out by working into the impressions seen through the gold leaf, followed by cleaning-off with the gold rubber. This method of tooling through a paper pattern is adopted also when complex decorative patterns are tooled.

Lettering in panels usually demands some care in the arrangement of space between, above and below lines of lettering. Traditional methods of spacing lines are as follows. For one line of lettering the height of the face to be used is subtracted from the height of the panel and the space remaining is divided into $1\frac{1}{3}$ parts above the line and $1\frac{2}{3}$ parts below the line of lettering.

For more than one line of lettering the height of the face to be used is multiplied by the number of lines and the total is subtracted from the height of the panel. The space remaining is divided into 1 part between each line of lettering, $1^{1/3}$ parts above the top line and $1^{2/3}$, parts below the bottom line. For example, where two lines of lettering are required, twice the height of face is subtracted from the height of the panel and the remaining space divided in 4 parts, one of the parts being divided into thirds for convenience when re-allocating the space for the lettering layout (i.e. $1^{1/3}$ 1 $^{2/3}$).

201

201   Metal edged pressing-boards are shown positioned in the french joints for the final pressing after the endpapers have been pasted-down. The inclusion of the thin card fence placed between the endpaper linings is usual when cloth-jointed endpapers are to be pressed. After pressing, the opening procedure shown in figures *93-94* is carried out. The leather is then polished with a soft duster and the quarter-leather library-style binding is completed.

APPENDIX 1   Paper

Standard British paper sizes in use before 1970:

Broadsheet	Size in inches
Foolscap	13½ x 17
Crown	15 x 20
Large Post	16½ x 21
Demy	17½ x 22½
Medium	18 x 23
Royal	20 x 25
Imperial	22 x 30

International Paper Sizes in use from 1970: A Series.

These are based on A0 (841 x 1189 mm), which is the equivalent of one square metre in area, and each subdivision or smaller size — A1, A2, A3, A4, etc, is half of the preceding larger size divided at its long edge. A feature of the series is that the proportions of adjacent sides to each other are constant in every size. If the shorter side is doubled or the longer halved, the new size is still in the same proportion.

A0	841 x 1189 mm
A1	594 x 841 mm
A2	420 x 594 mm
A3	297 x 420 mm
A4	210 x 297 mm
A5	148 x 210 mm
A6	105 x 148 mm

The stock sizes from which A series sizes can be cut or folded are:

RA0	860 x 1220 mm
RA1	610 x 860 mm
RA2	430 x 610 mm

Recommended standard book sizes:

A5	210 x 148 mm
Metric Crown 8vo	186 x 123 mm
Metric L. Crown 8vo	198 x 129 mm
Metric Demy 8vo	216 x 138 mm
Metric Royal 8vo	234 x 156 mm

Metric weights:
Paper is calculated by metric weight with price quotations per kilogram.
Substance:
Sheet substance is calculated in grammes per square metre.

APPENDIX 2 Board

Strawboard and millboard thicknesses:

Traditional Designation: Strawboard	Caliper Inches	Substance g/m^2
8 oz	0.027	500
12 oz	0.039	750
16 oz (1 lb)	0.052	1000
24 oz (1½ lb)	0.072	1400
32 oz (2 lb)	0.094	1900
40 oz (2½ lb)	0.121	2400

Traditional Designation: Millboard	Caliper Inches	Caliper Millimetres
6d	0.036	1.0
7d	0.048	1.2
8d	0.064	1.6
8d x	0.085	2.2
8d xx	0.116	2.9
10d (x)	0.144	3.6

APPENDIX 3
Covering materials

Woven Fabrics:
Bookcloth.
Cotton weave base cloth dressed and coloured. Matt, glazed, or embossed finishes. Sometimes paper backed. Water resistant library grades available. Traditionally the standard material for case bound work, now more particularly used for quality or special editions.

Buckram.
Cotton, union, or linen base. Stronger, heavier, and more durable than bookcloth, its distinctive weave is usually calendered to a smooth finish. Used where strength and an appearance of fine quality are demanded.

Art Canvas.
Exhibits a heavy open weave, is matt coloured and backed with paper. Its strength is comparable to buckram.

Crash Canvas.
Has a coarse weave and often an unbleached natural appearance. Is paper backed and very strong.

Fibre Felt:
Linson, Fabroleen, etc.
Strong paper-based covering materials. Embossed variously to simulate canvas, hopsack, linen etc. Some overprinted to improve the weave appearance. Water resistant library grades are available. Increasingly used in place of bookcloth, with which it is very competitive in terms of cost, strength, stability, appearance, and ease of working.

Leather:
Levant Morocco.
Large goatskins of approximately ten square feet in area, thick, strong, heavily grained, yet supple and easily worked if pared correctly. Expensive. Use restricted to fine bindings.

Niger Morocco.
Goatskins of approximately eight square feet in area. Light natural grains.

Oasis.
Nigerian goatskins and kids from four to eight square feet in area. Light natural grains of great beauty. Aniline dyed. Acid free and acid resistant. Generally the most popular leather for good quality hand bookbinding.

Hard-grain Morocco.
A common goatskin with small pin-head grain. Pigment coloured. Widely used in commercial hand binding.

Calf.
Calfskins are smooth and without noticeable grain. The best are acid free, acid resistant and aniline dyed. Sizes approximately ten square feet.

Sheepskin.
Plain sheepskins have a relatively smooth surface. Sometimes they are plate-grained in imitation of levant, hard-grain morocco etc. Less durable than the best goatskins, sheepskin can be difficult to pare and use. Its primary application is in stationery binding and in the cheaper classes of miscellaneous binding.

APPENDIX 4   Thread

Thread is sold by the reel, or in skeins and by weight. Suitable thicknesses of thread for general use are likely to be 25-2 cord (thin), 16-2 or 25-3 cord (medium) and 16-3 cord (thick). When a skein of thread is unknotted, it will be found to be in circular form; if the circle of thread is cut with shears at the point at which its two ends are knotted, it will produce single threads about 5 feet in length. These can be made into a plait (fig 7). Threads required for use should be pulled from the loop end of the plait rather than by their cut ends.

APPENDIX 5   Paste

Although commercially prepared paste can be obtained from suppliers, small quantities may be made as follows: Into a saucepan place 2 ounces of plain flour. Add slowly 1/2 pint of cold water while stirring with a wooden spoon. Bring to the boil, stirring continually as the mixture thickens. Remove from the stove. Add a pinch of crushed thymol crystals and beat well. The paste can be thinned with boiled water if necessary for a particular operation.

APPENDIX 6
Finishing Glaire

To Make:

1.   Beat one dessertspoonful of vinegar into the white of one large fresh egg. Allow to stand overnight and then strain through a piece of fine muslin before use.

2.   To one dessertspoonful of dried albumen, add four dessertspoonfuls of water and one of vinegar. Allow to stand overnight. Stir. Allow to settle and then strain through muslin.

Prepared:

Prepared shellac based glaire is available and it is applied similarly to egg glaire but without the need for a prior washing of leather with a vinegar solution. After application, this glaire should be allowed to dry for at least one hour. It can be tooled as normal and once applied to the cover material, its condition does not deteriorate, thus re-application of the glaire is not usually required.

APPENDIX 7   Some British and American terms compared

It would be difficult enough to establish a national standard of technical terms about which all bookbinders could agree, and necessarily even more difficult to compose tables of precisely equivalent terminology as used by craftsmen in two different countries, even though a common language exists between them.

The following is offered as an aid towards understanding. The lists are not comprehensive and are unlikely to be definitive.

British	American
Blocking	Stamping
Block	Die
Board cutter	Board shears
Card	Bristol Board
Carpenter's square	Right-angle gauge
Cartridge paper	Medium-grade book paper
Cotton-wool	Absorbent cotton
Cutting (of book edges)	Trimming
Fence	Barrier Sheet
G-Clamp	C-Clamp
Knocked-up	Jogged
Label cloth	Sized cambric
Millboard	Binder's Board
Mull	Super or crash
Plait	Braid
Paste-down (leaf of an end paper)	Board paper

SUPPLIERS OF EQUIPMENT AND MATERIAL

GREAT BRITAIN

Fibre-felt covering materials
The Grange Fibre Co. Ltd,
45 High Street, Hampton Wick,
Kingston-upon-Thames,
Surrey, KT1 4DG.

Leather
Harrold Leather Manufacturing Co. Ltd,
75 High Street, Harrold,
Beds, MK43 7BL.

Harmatan Leathers,
Block J, Penfold Works,
Imperial Way, Watford, Herts.

Equipment and sundries
Elizabeth McCraig,
Whitehill of Balmaghie, Bridge of Dee,
Castle Douglas, Kircudbrightshire,
Scotland.

Dryad Handicrafts,
178 Kensington High Street,
London, W8.

*Marble-paper, finishing stoves,
tool handles, and marbling inks*
Cockerell Bindery
Riversdale, Grantchester,
Cambridge, CB3 9NB

Adhesives
Croda Polymers Ltd,
153 New Bedford Road,
Luton, Beds, LU3 1LD.

Bookcloth
Red Bridge Book Cloth Co. Ltd,
Red Bridge Mill, Ainsworth,
Bolton, Lancs, BL2 5PD.

Winter & Co (London) Ltd,
Glebe Road,
Huntingdon,
Cambridgeshire, PE18 7DZ

*Leather, adhesives, bookcloth,
equipment, sundries*
J. Hewitt & Sons Ltd,
97 St John Street, London EC1
and 125 High Street, Edinburgh 1

Russell Bookcrafts, Bancroft,
Hitchin, Herts, SG5 1NF.

Handmade and decorative papers
Falkiner Fine Papers Ltd,
117 Long Acre, London WC2E 9PA.

Blocks and finishing tools
T. Mackrell and Co. Ltd,
Industrial Estate West,
Colchester Road, Witham,
Essex, CM8 3BB.

Fine-Cut Precision
Unit 8
Mill Road Industrial Estate
Southwick, Sussex, BN4 1PD.

Paper and strawboard
Spicer-Cowan Ltd,
Cavendish Road, Stevenage,
Herts, SG1 2EJ.

Gold leaf and foil
George M. Whiley Ltd,
Firth Road, Houston Industrial Estate,
Livingston, West Lothian, EH54 5DJ.

Millboard
Jackson's Millboard and Fibre Co. Ltd,
Bourne End, Bucks, SL8 5HJ.

USA

Equipment and sundries
Talas, 104 Fifth Avenue,
New York 10011.

Ernest Schaefer Co,
731 Leihigh Avenue, Union,
New Jersey 07083.

Leather, paper and sundries
Andrews-Nelson-Whitehead Inc,
7 Laight Street, New York

Tools and equipment
W. O. Hickok Manufacturing Co,
Ninth and Cumberland Streets,
Harrisburg, Pennsylvania.

Papers
Process Materials Corporation,
329 Veterans Boulevard, Carlstadt,
New Jersey 07072.

BIBLIOGRAPHY
Works on bookbinding history, design and technique

Burdett, Eric. *The Craft of Bookbinding*, David & Charles, Newton Abbot, 1975
Clements, Jeff. *Bookbinding*, Arco Publications, London, 1963.
Cockerell, Douglas. *Bookbinding and the Care of Books*, Pitman, London and New York, 1963.
Darley, Lionel. *Bookbinding Then and Now*, Faber, London, 1959.
Darley, Lionel. *Introduction to Bookbinding*, Faber, London, 1965.
Harthan, John P. *Victoria and Albert Museum: Bookbindings*, HMSO, London, 1961.
Horton, Carolyn. *Cleaning and Preserving Bindings and Related Materials*, American Library Association, Chicago, 1967.
Johnson, Arthur. *Bookbinding*, Thames & Hudson, London, 1978.
Johnson, Pauline. *Creative Bookbinding*, University of Washington Press, Washington, 1965.
McLean, Ruari. *Victorian Publishers' Book-bindings in Cloth and Leather*, Gordon Fraser London, 1974.
McLean, Ruari. *Victorian Publishers' Book-bindings in Paper*, Gordon Fraser London, 1983.
Mansfield, Edgar. *Modern Design in Bookbinding*, Peter Owen, London, 1966.
Middleton, Bernard C. *A History of English Craft Bookbinding Technique*, Halland Press, London, 1978.
Middleton, Bernard C. *The Restoration of Leather Bindings*, American Library Association, Chicago, 1972.
Smith, Philip. *New Directions in Bookbinding*, Studio Vista, London, 1974.
Vaughan, Alex J. *Modern Bookbinding*, Charles Skilton, London, 1960.

Index

124